ALTERNATOR BOOKS™

UNEXPLAINED

SPONTANEOUS HUMAN COMBUSTION

Craig Boutland

Lerner Publications ◆ Minneapolis

Lerner Publications Company
A division of Lerner Publishing Group, Inc.
241 First Avenue North
Minneapolis, MN 55401 USA

For reading levels and more information, look up this title at www.lernerbooks.com.

Main body text set in Minion Pro.
Font provided by Adobe Systems.

Library of Congress Cataloging-in-Publication Data

Names: Boutland, Craig, author.
Title: Spontaneous human combustion / Craig Boutland.
Description: Minneapolis : Lerner Publications, 2019. | Series: Unexplained
    (Alternator Books) | Audience: Age 8–12. | Audience: Grade 4 to 6. | Includes
    bibliographical references and index.
Identifiers: LCCN 2018054299 (print) | LCCN 2019015348 (ebook) | ISBN
    9781541562899 (eb pdf) | ISBN 9781541562837 (lb : alk. paper) | ISBN
    9781541573819 (pb : alk. paper)
Subjects: LCSH: Combustion, Spontaneous human—Juvenile literature.
Classification: LCC RA1085 (ebook) | LCC RA1085 .B68 2019 (print) | DDC 001.94—
    dc23

LC record available at https://lccn.loc.gov/2018054299

Manufactured in the United States of America
1-46409-47499-4/3/2019

Contents

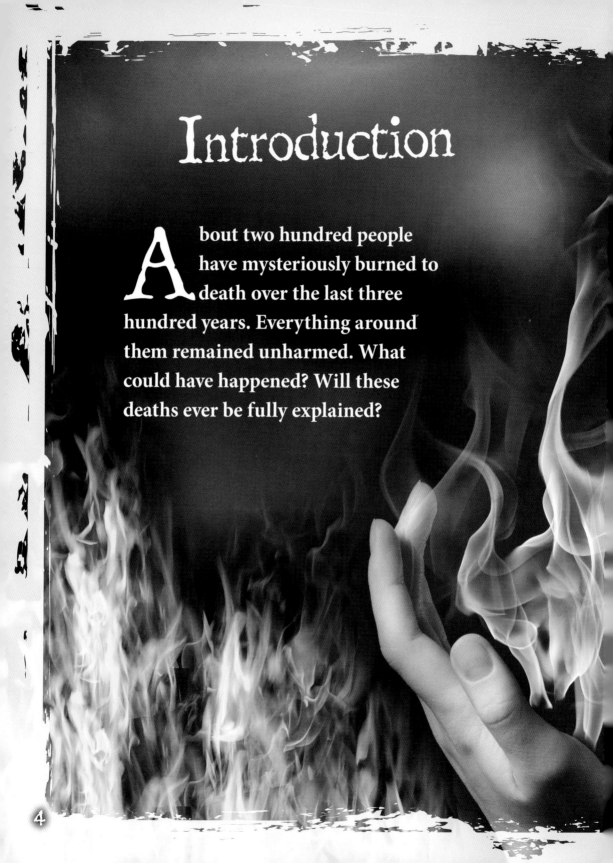

Introduction

About two hundred people have mysteriously burned to death over the last three hundred years. Everything around them remained unharmed. What could have happened? Will these deaths ever be fully explained?

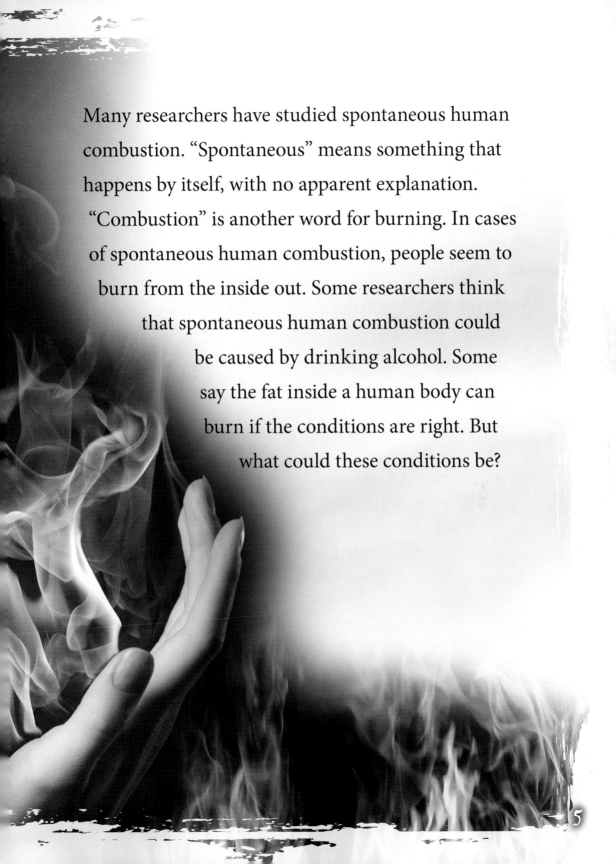

Many researchers have studied spontaneous human combustion. "Spontaneous" means something that happens by itself, with no apparent explanation. "Combustion" is another word for burning. In cases of spontaneous human combustion, people seem to burn from the inside out. Some researchers think that spontaneous human combustion could be caused by drinking alcohol. Some say the fat inside a human body can burn if the conditions are right. But what could these conditions be?

Countess di Bandi

In the early 1700s, an Italian priest named Giuseppe Bianchini described a story he had been told. Countess Cornelia di Bandi was sixty-two years old. She was found by her maid in her bedroom one morning. What the maid saw was distressing. She never forgot what she had seen.

The body of Countess di Bandi was lying on the floor between the bed and the window. Near the bed was a pile of ashes. The lower legs, from the knees to the feet, were not burned. The back of her head had been burned, but her face was recognizable. It was a **gruesome** sight.

Inside the Bedroom

There had been a small oil lamp and three candles burning in the room when the countess went to bed. When the maid entered the room, the oil lamp was empty. The candle wax had completely burned, but the candlewicks were untouched. There were ashes in the air and soot covered the room.

Countess Cornelia di Bandi lived and died in the Italian city of Cesena.

The bed and chest of drawers had not been burned. This was very strange. The fire must have been extremely fierce to have burned a body to ashes. In addition to the soot, there was only a wet, glue-like substance on the carpet, and a yellowish fluid was dripping down the lower part of the windows.

What Happened?

The priest Bianchini had a **theory**. The countess regularly bathed in a **flammable** liquid called camphor. It was used to help relieve aches and pains. Bianchini thought the camphor passed through the countess's skin to the fat **tissues** underneath. He guessed that di Bandi had left her bed to open the window and accidentally knocked over the oil lamp. The flame of the lamp **ignited** the flammable mixture inside her. No one knows for sure if this is what happened.

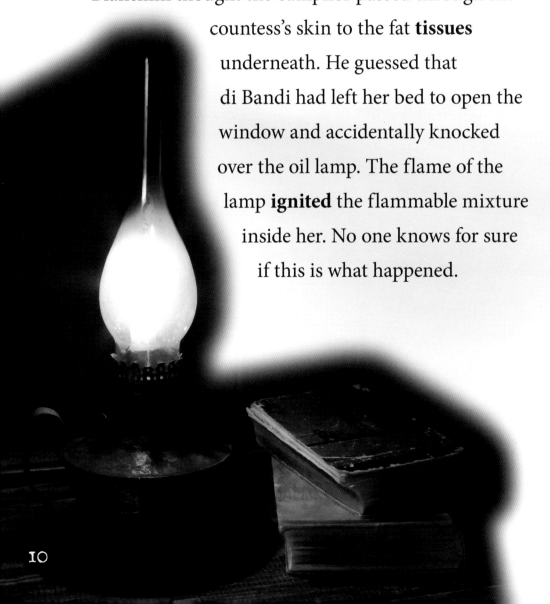

The death of Countess di Bandi was one of the first stories of spontaneous human combustion ever written down. There were other stories over the next one hundred years. When someone died in a fire, police officers had usually called it an accident. Sometimes they said the cause of death was "open," meaning there was no explanation. The term "spontaneous human combustion" was first used in British law courts to describe how some people might have died.

The Case Of Mary Reeser

T he most famous story of death by
spontaneous human combustion is that of
Mary Reeser. Mary lived alone in Florida.
Her burned body was found sitting in a chair at
her home in July 1951.

Weird Theories Pop Up In Reeser Death Puzzle

By JERRY BLIZIN

While police yesterday awaited FBI laboratory reports on the mystery death of Mrs. Mary Hardy Reeser, 67, an avalanche of theories from people in all walks of life continued to reach The Times and investigating authorities.

The body of Mrs. Reeser was reduced to ashes, except for one curiously intact foot, by a blaze at her apartment, 1200 Cherry Street Northeast, Monday. The fire did little other damage to the apartment and went unnoticed by the apartment owner, Mrs. P. M. Carpenter, or by other neighbors throughout the night.

One local resident, L. H. Horner, 3707 42nd Avenue North, wrote calling attention to the evidence of "spontaneous combustion of human bodies," as recorded by the late Charles Fort, who gained fame in past years for his delving into phenomena which science could not explain.

Other Cases

This reporter borrowed Horner's copy of "The Books of Charles Fort" and found repeated references to mysterious fires and deaths by fire.

Page 656 of Fort's works quotes from the London Daily News of Dec. 17, 1904: "Yesterday morning, Mrs. Thomas Cochrane, of Rosehall, Fallkirk, widow of a well-known local gentleman, was found burned to death in her bedroom . . burned almost beyond recognition . . little, if anything else burned . . body found sitting in a chair."

And again on page 928, Fort

"There was nothing to indicate the origin of the fire," the account reads, "the floor was burned under the body, but bedclothes, mattresses, curtains, all other things in the room, showed not a trace of fire. But this body was burned, as if it had been in the midst of flames of the intensity of a furnace."

The physician's report indicated that arms and hands, etc. had been reduced to cinders, but that no neighbor had heard any outcry.

Fort says that there is evidence for a peculiar kind of fire, sometimes called "spontaneous combustion of human bodies," which is restricted to one area and does not spread.

He also cites Dr. Dixon Mann's 1922 edition of "Forensic Medicine," where a report of a woman being burned to death and so consumed that only a pile of bones was found. Yet only three feet from the pile of cinders, is an unscorched cloth.

ST. PETERSBURG TIMES, THURSDAY, JULY 5, 1951

POLICE GET PLENTY OF ADVICE, BUT

No New Clues In Reeser Death; Debris Sent To L

By JERRY BLIZIN

Detectives yesterday finished packing the last of several of material salvaged from an apartment at 1200 Cherry Northeast, where Mrs. Mary Hardy Reeser, 67, was bur death in a mystery fire Monday.

The boxes will be sent off today to the FBI laboratory in Washington for chemical analysis. Included in the material sent are portions of the apartment rug, smoke samples, rubble from the walls and floor and segments of the chair in which Mrs. Reeser was last known to be sitting.

A BLAZE OF necessarily white - hot intensity disintegrated the body of Mrs. Reeser, a robust woman who weighed about 170 pounds. All that remained was a foot - curiously intact and without indication of charring, clad in a black houseshoe.

The shoe, previously identified as a suede shoe, yesterday was proven to be a black satin bedroom slipper.

Meanwhile Detective Chief Cass Burgess stated yesterday that he would wait until a chemical analysis report could be returned before making any statement as to what caused the blaze or what put it out.

"This fire is a curious thing," Burgess said, "and I've been deluged by letters and phone calls offering solutions to the problems facing us."

Magistrate Ed Silk, who acts as coroner in the case, yesterday said he'd received at least from amateur de-

BURGESS SAID an u letter arrived yesterday ing addressed to "Chel tectiffs." "The letter said ball of fire came thro open window and hit he it happen."

Silk reported that P told him a kapok cush overstuffed chair did while others put the er, kerosene, nap ether, thermite bombs fire), thermite bombs um and phosphorus.

Almost all of t said, odor not d Apar

Silk death Reeser death gin. "tent vesti

con m is bu at

letters sent The

Newspapers reporting the death of
Mary Reeser printed possible answers to
the mystery alongside other stories of
spontaneous human combustion.

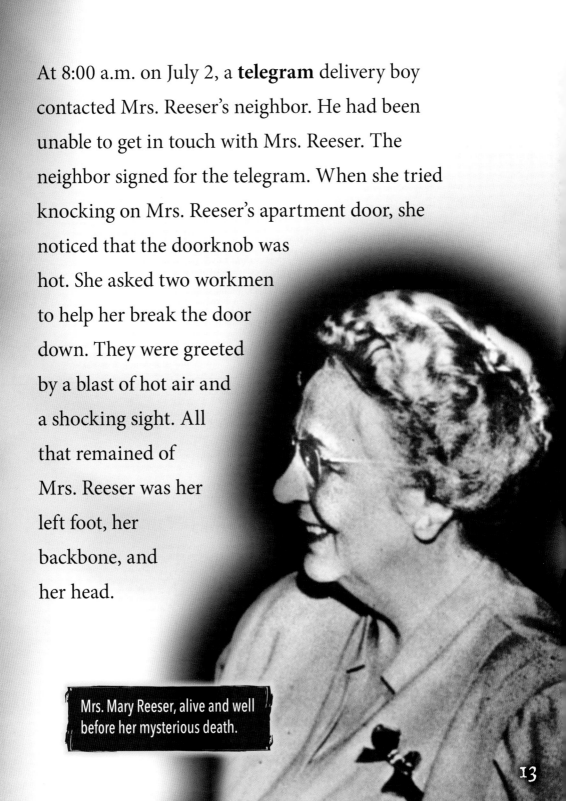

At 8:00 a.m. on July 2, a **telegram** delivery boy contacted Mrs. Reeser's neighbor. He had been unable to get in touch with Mrs. Reeser. The neighbor signed for the telegram. When she tried knocking on Mrs. Reeser's apartment door, she noticed that the doorknob was hot. She asked two workmen to help her break the door down. They were greeted by a blast of hot air and a shocking sight. All that remained of Mrs. Reeser was her left foot, her backbone, and her head.

Mrs. Mary Reeser, alive and well before her mysterious death.

Police went through the ashes of Mary Reeser's armchair looking for evidence.

The top halves of the walls were covered with soot. A mirror had cracked, and a plastic cup and two candles had melted. The chair Mrs. Reeser had been sitting on had been destroyed. But the rest of the room was untouched. How had her body been so badly burned while the room itself had very little damage?

Experts had many theories about what might
have killed Mary. Some thought she had been hit
by **ball lightning** or a **fireball**. Others suggested that
her body produced a flammable gas and exploded.
The police thought she had been smoking and fallen
asleep. They guessed that her cigarette ignited her
nightgown and started the fire.

It seems very unlikely that Mary
Reeser was killed by a fireball.
It would have set fire to her entire
apartment. But it was one theory.

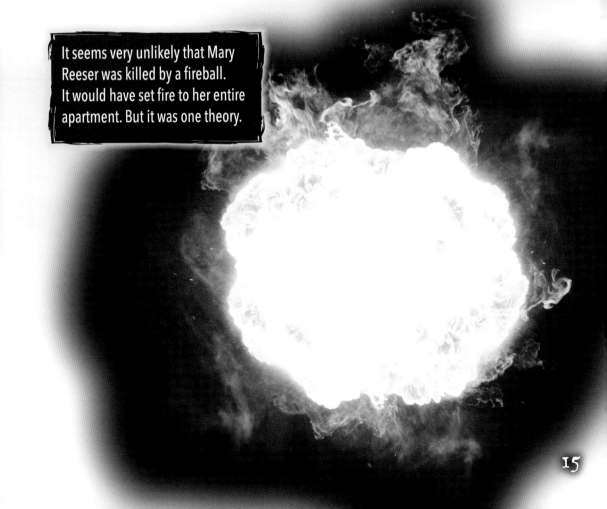

No Further Clues

The police were still **mystified**. They couldn't explain what had happened after Mary's nightgown had caught fire. The police wanted to know how a fire strong enough to burn a human body could be **confined** to such a small area. The heat must have been intense. Police estimated that the temperature had reached 3,500°F (1,930°C).

Black Magic?

The police asked Professor Wilton M. Krogman
of the University of Pennsylvania to look at the
room. He had investigated many other deaths caused
by fire. He said that the scene in the room was the
most incredible thing he had ever seen. He suggested
that if this had happened a few hundred years ago,
people would have blamed it on black magic.

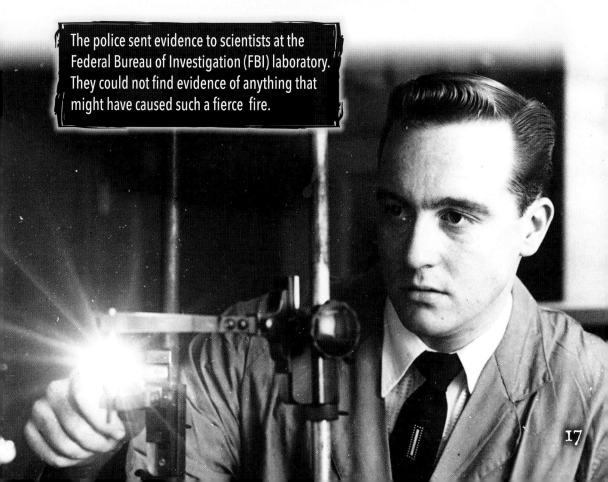

The police sent evidence to scientists at the
Federal Bureau of Investigation (FBI) laboratory.
They could not find evidence of anything that
might have caused such a fierce fire.

Possible Explanations

In the twenty-first century there have been more mysterious deaths by burning. In 2010, for example, a court in Ireland recorded the death of a man by spontaneous combustion. The report added that although the fire had been thoroughly investigated, there was no explanation for it. In 2017 a man suddenly burst into flames on a street in London, England. He may have set himself on fire while trying to light a cigarette. But why had he burned so quickly?

Since the case of the Countess di Bandi in the 1700s, many theories for spontaneous human combustion have been suggested. In southern Germany in the 1800s, many cases were linked to drinking alcohol. But was the alcohol responsible for setting fire to people's clothing? Or is a more likely explanation that people did not notice the flames until it was too late?

Methane Gas

There was another theory for these strange deaths. Some people thought that natural gases inside the body caught fire. Flammable gases like methane can be found in the stomachs of people who have recently died. Doctors in a London hospital wrote about such a case in 1885. After a man died in the hospital, his body seemed to inflate. The doctors made a small cut in his stomach. When they did, gas came out and ignited.

The doctors suggested that if this man had died in his own house, instead of in the hospital, the gas inside his body could have caught fire. The death would have been reported as a case of spontaneous human combustion. Some haystacks can catch fire in a similar way. When bacteria inside the haystack grow, they create methane gas, which can spontaneously catch fire.

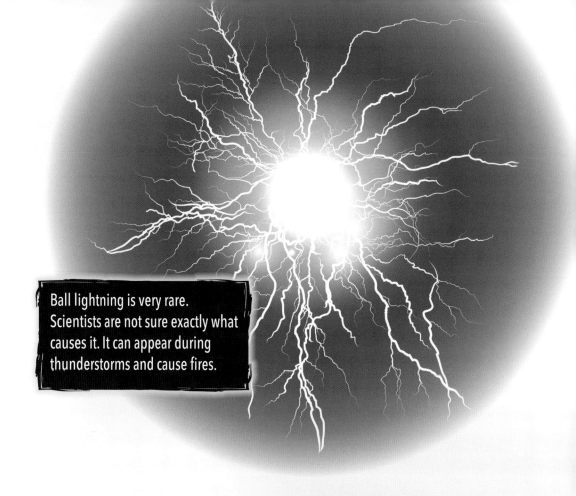

Ball lightning is very rare. Scientists are not sure exactly what causes it. It can appear during thunderstorms and cause fires.

Some researchers do not believe that alcohol or gases cause spontaneous human combustion. They think something outside the body causes extreme rises in temperature. One explanation, they say, is ball lightning. This can strike suddenly, raising temperatures to dangerously high levels. However, there is no evidence that ball lightning was the cause of any of the reported deaths.

Mind Power

Our minds play an important role in controlling our bodies. Some researchers think that mental stress may make people catch fire. Other researchers believe there are lines through the earth that carry a mysterious energy that affects people's minds. One writer believed that there was a new **subatomic particle** called the pyrotron that caused people to burst into flames.

The Wick Effect?

The cases of death by spontaneous combustion are similar. The person usually lives alone. Feet and hands are often left unburned. The fire does not cause any other major damage. Any ashes are often greasy and smell bad. There was usually a flame nearby, such as an open fire or a lit cigarette. These could have provided the spark that set off the blaze.

In 1980 a man was found burned to death in Wales. It was a typical case. All that remained were his legs below the knee and his skull. Half the chair he was sitting in had been destroyed, but nothing else in the room had burned. Investigators decided that he had died because of something they called the wick effect.

Human Candle

Researchers use the wick effect as a possible explanation for spontaneous human combustion. If a person is asleep, a spark from a fire source could drop onto their clothes. A small fire starts and splits the person's skin. This releases fat tissues that soak into the person's clothing. The flame then burns up the fat-soaked clothing at a slow, steady pace.

While the clothing burns, more fat is released from the body. Most people have enough fat stored to keep a fire going if help is not nearby. The slow burning evaporates water in the body that would otherwise stop the body from burning completely.

Although the theory seems **convincing**, the burning process is a slow one. People who have died from spontaneous human combustion are reported to have burned in minutes. The only other likely explanation may be the chemical **acetone**. This substance is produced in tiny amounts in the human body. Acetone burns at a high temperature that could ignite the fat in the body.

Do You Believe?

There are many theories about spontaneous human combustion. But what causes some people to burn to death unexpectedly is still a mystery. Is it chemicals inside the body? Is it the wick effect?

We do not know if spontaneous combustion is possible. But we do know that many people believe that it is.

Glossary

acetone: a flammable liquid used to dissolve or make chemical compounds, often found in nail polish remover

confined: kept to a small area

convincing: capable of persuading a person that something is true or real

fireball: a meteor with bright sparks that form a tail behind it

flammable: a substance that is easily set on fire, or which catches fire easily

gruesome: causing horror or disgust

ignited: caught fire or caused to catch fire

mystified: to be completely confused by something

subatomic particle: a tiny particle smaller than an atom

telegram: a message from a telegraph, a device that used coded signals to communicate over long distances

theory: an idea that is used to explain or justify something, the starting point of an argument or investigation

tissues: a mass or layer of cells that form the basic structural materials of a plant or animal

Further Information

Is Spontaneous Human Combustion Real?
https://www.history.com/news/is-spontaneous-human-combustion-real

Claybourne, Anna. *Don't Read This Book Before Bed: Thrills, Chills, and Hauntingly True Stories*. London: National Geographic Kids, 2017.

How Stuff Works: Spontaneous Human Combustion
https://science.howstuffworks.com/science-vs-myth/unexplained-phenomena/shc.htm

Martineau, Susan. *Real-Life Mysteries.* Kew, United Kingdom: b small publishing, 2017.

Shea, Therese. *Freaky Weather Stories*. New York: Gareth Stevens, 2016.

Safe Kids Worldwide: Fire Safety
https://www.safekids.org/fire

Spontaneous Human Combustion: Theories
http://spontaneoushumancombustionmm.weebly.com/theories.html

Index

Photo Acknowledgments

The images inside this book are used with permission of: ©Shutterstock/donates, p. 1; ©Shutterstock/Konstantin Yuganov, p. 4-5; ©Public Domain/STFMIC, p. 6-7; ©Shutterstock/Lullia Beliaeva, p. 8; ©Shutterstock/Gone with the Wind, p. 9; ©iStockphoto.com/EvBuh, p. 10; ©iStockphoto.com/gregobagel, p. 11; ©Public Domain/St Petersburg Times/Floridazone, p. 12; ©Topfoto/Fortean, p. 13; ©Topfoto/Fortean, p. 14; ©iStockphoto.com/ramihilm, p. 15; ©iStockphoto.com/SK Howard, p. 16; ©Public Domain/FBI Photos, p. 17; ©iStockphoto.com/Pavliha, p. 18-19; ©Shutterstock/Sebos, p. 20; ©Shutterstock/Tramp57, p. 21; ©Shutterstock/Snowboard School, p. 22; ©Shutterstock/Mariav, p. 23; ©Shutterstock/FamencodiabioPhotography, p. 24-25; ©iStockphoto.com/Liudmyar Supynska, p. 27; ©Shutterstock/twobee, p. 28-29.

Front Cover: ©Shutterstock/Vibrant Image Studio

Brown Bear Books has made every attempt to contact the copyright holder. If anyone has any information please contact licensing@brownbear.co.uk